P9-DMJ-846

WILLIAMS-SONOMA

FOODMADEFAST
SOUP

RECIPES
Georgeanne Brennan

GENERAL EDITOR
Chuck Williams

PHOTOGRAPHY
Bill Bettencourt

Oxmoor House®

contents

30 MINUTES START TO FINISH

about this book

Today, we care more than ever about the food we eat. Yet we have less time than ever to cook. *Soup* unlocks the secret to putting delicious homemade meals on the table with a minimum of time and labor. The recipes in this book have been carefully crafted to make the most of a few well-chosen ingredients in order to create a satisfying meal based around soup.

In these pages, you'll find both traditional and contemporary recipes, many of which can be made in less than 20 minutes. Buttery Roasted Garlic Soup and Crab & Avocado Soup are both made with just seven or fewer ingredients and ten minutes of hands-on time. You'll find international favorites, too, from Vietnamese Beef Noodle Soup to slow-cooked French Onion Soup. Add a loaf of crusty bread and a salad or side dish and you've got a delicious home-cooked meal that demands surprisingly little effort to put on the table.

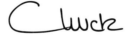

30 minutes
start to finish

creamy
spinach soup

Unsalted butter,
2 tablespoons

Yellow onion, ¼, finely
chopped

Garlic, 1 clove, minced

Chicken broth, 4 cups
(32 fl oz/1 l)

Day-old baguette, 2 slices

Baby spinach, 4 cups
(4 oz/125 g), packed

Heavy (double) cream,
¼ cup (2 fl oz/60 ml), plus
more for drizzling

Lemon zest, from 1 lemon,
finely grated

**Salt and freshly ground
pepper**

SERVES 4

1 Sauté the onion and garlic
In a large saucepan over medium heat, melt the butter.
Add the onion and sauté until translucent, 3–4 minutes. Add
the garlic and sauté for 1 minute longer.

2 Cook the spinach
Add the broth and the bread slices, reduce the heat
to low, cover, and simmer for 10 minutes. Add the spinach and
continue to simmer until the spinach is wilted and bright green,
about 5 minutes longer.

3 Purée the soup
Using a food processor or blender, process the soup
to a smooth purée. Return to the pan. Add the ¼ cup cream and
the lemon zest and reheat to serving temperature. Season
to taste with salt and pepper. Ladle the soup into bowls. Drizzle
with cream and serve.

cook's tip

Instead of the spinach, you can use 2 cups (4 oz/125 g) chopped kale or Swiss chard. Before chopping the leaves, remove the tough stems. Increase the cooking time by 30 minutes for kale or by 15 minutes for chard.

cook's tip

For additional flavor, garnish the soup with 1 tablespoon chopped fresh dill or ½ cup (1 oz/30 g) chopped baby arugula (rocket).

greek chicken-lemon soup

1 Cook the rice and chicken
Prepare the rice according to the package directions and set aside. Meanwhile, in a saucepan over medium-high heat, bring the broth to a simmer. Add the chicken, reduce the heat to low, and simmer, uncovered, until the chicken is cooked through, about 7 minutes. Remove the pan from the heat and set aside.

2 Make the lemon-egg mixture
In a small bowl, stir together the cornstarch and 1 tablespoon water until combined. In a small saucepan over low heat, whisk together the egg yolks and lemon juice. When just warm, whisk in the cornstarch mixture, and then 1 cup (8 fl oz/250 ml) of the broth from the chicken. Raise the heat to medium and continue to whisk until a thick sauce has formed, about 5 minutes. Season to taste with salt and pepper.

3 Finish the soup
Return the pan holding the broth and chicken to medium heat and bring to a simmer. Add the lemon-egg mixture while whisking continuously; the soup will thicken slightly. Stir in the rice and season to taste with salt and pepper. Ladle the soup into bowls and serve.

Long-grain rice, 1 cup (7 oz/220 g)

Chicken broth, 3 cups (24 fl oz/750 ml)

Boneless, skinless chicken thighs or breasts, about 1½ lb (750 g), cut into bite-sized pieces

Cornstarch (cornflour), 1 teaspoon

Egg yolks, 3

Lemon juice, from ½ lemon

Salt and freshly ground pepper

SERVES 4

pork & soba noodle soup

Canola or peanut oil,
2 tablespoons

Boneless pork loin chops,
2, cut into slices ¼ inch
(6 mm) thick

Fresh ginger, 1 tablespoon,
grated

Garlic, 2 cloves, thinly sliced

Yellow onion, ¼, finely
chopped

Soy sauce, 1 tablespoon

Chicken broth, 6 cups
(48 fl oz/1.5 l)

Dried soba noodles,
½ lb (250 g)

Button mushrooms,
4, thinly sliced

Green (spring) onions,
4, white and pale green
parts, thinly sliced

**Salt and freshly ground
pepper**

SERVES 4

1 Sauté the pork
In a small frying pan over medium heat, warm the oil.
When it is hot, add the pork and sauté until golden brown,
about 4 minutes. Add the ginger, garlic, yellow onion, and soy
sauce and sauté until the onion is translucent, about 2 minutes
longer. Remove from the heat and set aside.

2 Cook the soba noodles
In a large saucepan over medium-high heat, bring the
broth to a boil. Add the soba and stir to separate the noodles.
Cook just until tender, about 5 minutes. Add the pork mixture,
mushrooms, and green onions and cook for 1 minute to heat
through. Season to taste with salt and pepper. Ladle into
bowls and serve.

cook's tip

To peel and grate fresh ginger, first remove the skin with a vegetable peeler. Then grate the peeled ginger on a fine rasp grater or the finest rasps of a box grater-shredder.

cook's tip

If desired, you can use the meat of 2 lb (1 kg) freshly steamed clams. Discard any clams that fail to close to the touch, then steam them in a wide, covered saucepan with 1 cup (8 fl oz/250 ml) water until they open. Discard any clams that do not open. Let cool, then remove the meat from the shells.

clam
chowder

1 Cook the bacon and vegetables

In a large saucepan over medium heat, cook the bacon, stirring often, until it starts to brown and has rendered some of its fat, about 3 minutes. Using a slotted spoon, transfer to paper towels to drain. Add the butter to the bacon drippings. When it melts, add the celery, onion, thyme, and bay leaf and sauté until the onion is translucent, about 2 minutes. Add the potatoes and stir well. Add the reserved clam liquor and 2 cups (16 fl oz/500 ml) water and bring to a boil. Reduce the heat to low, cover, and simmer until the potatoes are tender, about 15 minutes.

2 Finish the soup

Add the milk and cream and stir to combine. Add the clam meat, heat through, and season to taste with salt and pepper. Remove and discard the bay leaf. Ladle the chowder into individual bowls, garnish with the bacon, and serve.

Bacon, 3 slices, chopped

Unsalted butter,
1 tablespoon

Celery, 2 stalks, chopped

Yellow onion, ¼, finely chopped

Dried thyme, ½ teaspoon

Bay leaf, 1

Red potatoes, 3, cubed

Clam meat, 2 cans (6½ oz/ 200 g each), chopped, plus reserved clam liquor

Milk, 1½ cups (12 fl oz/ 375 ml)

Heavy (double) cream,
1 cup (8 fl oz/250 ml)

Salt and freshly ground pepper

SERVES 4

cauliflower soup

Unsalted butter,
2 tablespoons

Yellow onion, ¼, chopped

Garlic, 2 cloves, minced

Chicken broth, 4 cups
(32 fl oz/1 l)

Dry white wine, ½ cup
(4 fl oz/125 ml)

Cauliflower, 1 medium
head, trimmed and coarsely
chopped

Heavy (double) cream,
¼ cup (2 fl oz/60 ml)

**Salt and freshly ground
pepper**

Paprika, ½ teaspoon

SERVES 4

1 Sauté the onion and garlic
In a large saucepan over medium heat, melt the butter.
Add the onion and the garlic and sauté until nearly translucent,
about 2 minutes.

2 Simmer the cauliflower
Add the broth, wine, and cauliflower, raise the heat
to medium-high, and bring to a boil. Reduce the heat to low
and simmer gently, uncovered, until the cauliflower is tender,
about 20 minutes.

3 Purée the soup
Using a food processor or blender, process the soup
to a smooth purée. Return to the pan. Place over medium heat,
stir in the cream, and reheat to serving temperature. Season
to taste with salt and pepper. Ladle into bowls, sprinkle with
the paprika, and serve.

cook's tip

For an easy cauliflower-cheese soup, stir in 1 cup (4 oz/125 g) shredded Cheddar or Monterey jack cheese just before ladling into bowls in step 3. Garnish with a scattering of croutons.

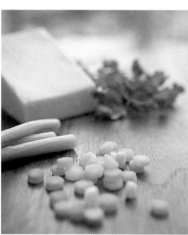

cook's tip

Other garnishing ideas for this
soup include shredded sharp
Cheddar or Monterey jack cheese,
chopped fresh cilantro (fresh
coriander), or thinly sliced green
(spring) onions.

spicy black bean soup

1 Cook the bacon and vegetables

In a large saucepan over medium heat, cook the bacon until the fat is rendered, about 5 minutes. Add the onion and sauté until translucent, about 2 minutes. Stir in the garlic, tomato, cumin, chili powder, chipotle chiles, and red wine vinegar.

2 Simmer the soup

Add the beans, broth, and 1 teaspoon salt. Raise the heat to high and bring to a boil. Reduce the heat to low and simmer, partially covered, to heat through and blend the flavors, about 10 minutes. In a blender or food processor, purée 1–2 cups (8–16 fl oz/250–500 ml) of the soup, then return to the pan and reheat to serving temperature. Season to taste with salt and pepper. Ladle the soup into bowls, garnish with the sour cream, and serve.

Bacon, 4 slices, cut into ½-inch (12-mm) pieces

Yellow onion, ½, finely chopped

Garlic, 3 cloves, minced

Tomato, 1 large, chopped

Ground cumin, 1 teaspoon

Chili powder, 1 teaspoon

Chipotle chiles in adobo, 2, finely chopped

Red wine vinegar, 1 tablespoon

Black beans, 2 cans (14½ oz/455 g each), drained and rinsed

Chicken broth, 6 cups (48 fl oz/1.5 l)

Salt and freshly ground pepper

Sour cream, ¼ cup (2 oz/ 60 g), for garnish

SERVES 4

21

mussels with fennel-herb broth

Unsalted butter,
1 tablespoon

Olive oil, 1 tablespoon

Yellow onion, ½, finely chopped

Garlic, 3 cloves, minced

Fennel bulb, 1 small, trimmed and chopped

Dry white wine, 1½ cups (12 fl oz/375 ml)

Fish stock, 2 cups (16 fl oz/ 500 ml)

Mussels, 5 lb (2.5 kg), scrubbed and debearded if necessary

Dried thyme, 1 teaspoon

Salt and freshly ground pepper

SERVES 4–6

1 Sauté the vegetables
In a large saucepan over medium-high heat, melt the butter with the oil. Add the onion, garlic, and fennel and sauté until the onion is translucent, 2–3 minutes.

2 Steam the mussels
Add the wine, fish stock, and mussels, discarding any mussels that fail to close to the touch. Sprinkle the thyme over the mussels. Cover, reduce the heat to low, and cook just until the mussels open, 10–12 minutes. Divide the mussels among shallow bowls, discarding any that failed to open. Season the broth to taste with salt and pepper, ladle into the bowls, and serve.

cook's tip

Today, most mussels are farm raised and have only small or no beards—the tuft of fibers they use to hold onto rocks or pilings. To remove a beard, scrape or cut it away with a knife or scissors, or firmly pull down, toward the shell's hinge end, with your fingertips.

cook's tip

Sautéed leeks are a flavorful base
for many soups and stews. For
a classic potato-leek soup, simply
omit the bacon and the sharp
Cheddar cheese.

potato-cheddar soup

1 Cook the bacon and vegetables

In a large saucepan over medium heat, cook the bacon until crisp, about 5 minutes. Transfer the bacon to paper towels to drain. Discard all but 2 tablespoons of the bacon drippings from the pan and return to medium heat. Add the leek and sauté until translucent, about 2 minutes. Add the cubed potatoes and the broth and stir. Bring to a boil, then reduce the heat to low. Cook, covered, until the potatoes are tender, about 15 minutes.

2 Purée the soup

Raise the heat to medium, add the milk and ½ teaspoon pepper, and bring just to a simmer. Using a food processor or blender, process the soup to a smooth purée. Return to the saucepan and reheat to serving temperature. Add the cheese and stir until melted. Season to taste with salt and pepper. Ladle the soup into bowls, crumble the bacon on top, and serve.

Bacon, 4 slices

Leek, 1, white part only, halved, rinsed, and thinly sliced

Russet potatoes, 3 large, peeled and cubed

Chicken broth, 2 cups (16 fl oz/500 ml)

Milk, 3 cups (24 fl oz/ 750 ml)

Salt and freshly ground pepper

Sharp Cheddar cheese, ½ cup (2 oz/60 g) shredded

SERVES 4

florentine white bean soup

Olive oil, 2 tablespoons

Pancetta or bacon, 3 oz (90 g), chopped

Yellow onion, 1 small, finely chopped

Carrots, 2, finely chopped

Garlic, 2 cloves, minced

Dried oregano, ½ teaspoon

Tomato paste, 1 tablespoon

Chicken broth, 4 cups (32 fl oz/1 l)

Cannellini beans, 2 cans (14½ oz/455 g each), drained and rinsed

Baby spinach, 2 cups (2 oz/60 g), chopped

Salt and freshly ground pepper

Fresh flat-leaf (Italian) parsley, 2 tablespoons minced

SERVES 4

1 Sauté the vegetables

In a large saucepan over medium-low heat, warm the oil. When it is hot, add the pancetta and sauté until it browns slightly, about 5 minutes. Raise the heat to medium, add the onion and carrots, and sauté until the vegetables are soft, about 5 minutes. Add the garlic and oregano and cook, stirring occasionally, until fragrant, about 2 minutes.

2 Finish the soup

Stir in the tomato paste, mixing well. Add the broth and the beans. Raise the heat to medium-high and bring to a boil, then reduce the heat to medium. Add the spinach and cook until it is wilted and the flavors have blended, about 10 minutes. Season to taste with salt and pepper. Ladle the soup into bowls, sprinkle with the parsley, and serve.

cook's tip

To cut kernels from an ear of corn,
break or cut the ear in half
crosswise. Using a sharp knife, cut
straight down between the cob
and the kernels, rotating the ear
a quarter turn after each cut.

sausage, corn & clam soup

1 Brown the sausage and vegetables

In a large saucepan or Dutch oven over medium-high heat, warm the oil. When it is hot, add the sausage and sauté until browned, about 5 minutes. Add the onion and garlic and sauté for 1 minute longer.

2 Cook the potatoes

Add the tomatoes, broth, oregano, and potatoes and bring to a boil. Reduce the heat to low, cover, and simmer until the potatoes are tender, about 15 minutes.

3 Cook the corn and clams

Add the corn and clams, discarding any clams that fail to close to the touch. Raise the heat to medium, cover, and cook until the clams open and the corn is tender, about 5 minutes. Remove from the heat and let stand, covered, for 5 minutes. Season to taste with salt and pepper. Ladle the soup into individual bowls, discarding any clams that failed to open, and serve.

Olive oil, 1 tablespoon

Sweet Italian sausages, 2, cut into slices ½ inch (12 mm) thick

Yellow onion, ¼, chopped

Garlic, 1 clove, minced

Canned whole plum (Roma) tomatoes, ½ cup (3 oz/90 g) drained and chopped

Chicken broth, 4 cups (32 fl oz/1 l)

Dried oregano, 1 teaspoon

Russet potatoes, 2, peeled and cut into small cubes

Corn kernels, 1½ cups (9 oz/280 g), fresh or frozen

Clams, such as littleneck, 1 lb (500 g), scrubbed

Salt and freshly ground pepper

SERVES 4

thai chicken-coconut soup

Orange, 1 small

Coconut milk, 3 cups
(24 fl oz/750 ml)

Chicken broth, 1 ½ cups
(12 fl oz/375 ml)

Asian fish sauce,
2 teaspoons

**Boneless, skinless chicken
breast halves,** 2, cut into
bite-sized pieces

Button mushrooms,
6 oz (185 g), quartered

Lime juice, from 1 lime

**Salt and freshly ground
pepper**

**Fresh basil, preferably
Thai,** ¼ cup (⅓ oz/10 g)
chopped

SERVES 4

1 Make the soup base

Grate 1 tablespoon zest and extract ½ cup (4 fl oz/
125 ml) juice from the orange and set aside. In a large
saucepan over medium-high heat, combine the orange juice
and zest, coconut milk, broth, and fish sauce. Stir well and
bring to a boil.

2 Cook the chicken and mushrooms

Reduce the heat to low, add the chicken, and simmer,
uncovered, for 5 minutes. Add the mushrooms and continue
to cook until the chicken is opaque throughout and the
mushrooms are tender, about 5 minutes longer. Add the lime
juice and season to taste with salt and pepper. Ladle into
bowls, garnish with the basil, and serve.

cook's tip

For a spicier soup, add 2 seeded
and minced Thai or serrano chiles.
Use kitchen gloves to protect
your hands while mincing and
seeding chiles, as they have
volatile oils that will irritate
your skin.

cook's tip

For a heartier soup that resembles
a quick version of gumbo, ladle
each serving of soup over a scoop
of cooked long-grain rice.

cajun shrimp soup

1 Make the soup base

In a large saucepan over medium-high heat, warm the oil. When it is hot, add the onion and sauté until translucent, about 2 minutes. Stir in the garlic and bell pepper, and then add the chile, tomatoes, broth, thyme, and cayenne. Bring to a boil, reduce the heat to low, and simmer, uncovered, until the flavors have blended, about 15 minutes.

2 Cook the shrimp

Add the shrimp and the filé powder and cook just until the shrimp turn pink and opaque, about 3 minutes. Season to taste with salt and black pepper. Ladle into bowls and serve.

Olive oil, 2 tablespoons

Yellow onion, ¼, finely chopped

Garlic, 2 cloves, minced

Green bell pepper (capsicum), ½, seeded and finely chopped

Serrano chile, 1, seeded and finely chopped

Canned whole plum (Roma) tomatoes, 2 cups (16 fl oz/500 ml), chopped, with juice

Chicken broth, 2 cups (16 fl oz/500 ml)

Fresh thyme, ½ teaspoon minced

Cayenne pepper, ¼ teaspoon

Shrimp (prawns), 1 lb (500 g), peeled and deveined

Filé powder, ½ teaspoon

Salt and freshly ground black pepper

SERVES 4

33

cucumber soup

Cucumbers, 3, peeled

Plain yogurt, 1½ cups
(12 oz/375 g)

Fresh mint, 2 tablespoons
chopped

Garlic, 1 clove, minced

Yellow onion, ½, coarsely
chopped

White country bread,
1 large slice, crust removed,
cubed

Chicken broth, ½ cup
(4 fl oz/125 ml)

Salt and white pepper

SERVES 4

1 **Prepare the cucumbers**
Cut each cucumber in half lengthwise. Using a
teaspoon, scoop out and discard the seeds. Roughly chop
2½ of the cucumbers. Finely chop the remaining cucumber
half and reserve for garnish.

2 **Purée the soup**
In a food processor or blender, combine the cucumbers,
yogurt, 1 tablespoon of the mint, the garlic, onion, bread, and
broth. Process to a smooth purée. Season to taste with salt
and white pepper.

3 **Garnish the soup**
Serve at once or, for a chilled soup, transfer to an airtight
container and refrigerate for 2–8 hours. Ladle the soup into
bowls. Garnish with the reserved cucumber and the remaining
mint and serve.

cook's tip

To chill soup quickly, fill a large
bowl or your sink with ice water.
Pour the puréed soup into a
smaller bowl and nest in the ice.
Stir the soup occasionally to
hasten the cooling.

spicy gazpacho

1 **Make the soup**
In a food processor or blender, combine half of the tomatoes, cucumber, bell pepper, and onion with all of the chiles and garlic. Process to a coarse paste. Add half of the cilantro and all of the olive oil, tomato juice, and red wine vinegar and process to a smooth purée. Season to taste with salt and pepper.

2 **Garnish the soup**
Serve at once or, for a chilled soup, transfer to an airtight container and refrigerate for 2–8 hours or up to 2 days. Ladle the soup into bowls. Garnish with the remaining tomatoes, cucumber, bell pepper, onion, and cilantro and the croutons, and serve.

Plum (Roma) tomatoes, 8, chopped

Cucumber, 1, peeled, halved, seeded, and chopped

Red bell pepper (capsicum), 1 small, seeded and chopped

Red onion, 1 small, chopped

Serrano chiles, 2, seeded

Garlic, 2 cloves

Fresh cilantro (fresh coriander), ½ cup (¾ oz/ 20 g) chopped

Olive oil, 1 tablespoon

Tomato juice, 1 ½ cups (12 fl oz/375 ml), chilled

Red wine vinegar, 2 tablespoons

Salt and freshly ground pepper

Croutons, 1 ½ cups (2 ½ oz/75 g)

SERVES 4

curried carrot soup

Olive oil, 1 tablespoon, plus more for drizzling

Shallot, 1 large, minced

Carrots, 1 ½ lb (750 g), coarsely chopped

Curry powder, 1 teaspoon

Chicken broth, 6 cups (48 fl oz/1.5 l)

Fresh orange juice, 2 tablespoons

Salt and freshly ground pepper

SERVES 4

1 Make the soup

In a large saucepan over medium heat, warm the 1 tablespoon oil. When it is hot, add the shallot and sauté until translucent, about 2 minutes. Add the carrots, curry powder, and broth. Raise the heat to medium-high and bring to a boil. Reduce the heat to low, cover, and cook until the carrots are tender, about 20 minutes. Remove from the heat and add the orange juice. Using a food processor or blender, process to a smooth purée. Season to taste with salt and pepper.

2 Garnish the soup

The soup can be served warm or chilled. To serve warm, return the puréed soup to the saucepan and gently warm over medium heat. To serve chilled, let cool, transfer to an airtight container, and refrigerate for 2–8 hours. Ladle into bowls, drizzle with oil, sprinkle with pepper, and serve.

cook's tip

Good-quality chicken stock can often be found in the freezer section of upscale markets, delis, and some butchers.

cook's tip

If the avocados that you have
purchased are too firm, put them
into a paper bag with an apple
or a banana. The ethylene gas
naturally emitted by either fruit
will hasten ripening.

crab &
avocado soup

1 Make the soup
In a food processor or blender, combine the avocados, chiles, coconut milk, lime juice, and ¾ cup (6 fl oz/180 ml) water and process to a smooth purée. Season to taste with salt, white pepper, and additional lime juice.

2 Garnish the soup
Serve at once or, for a chilled soup, transfer to an airtight container and refrigerate for 2–8 hours. Ladle the soup into individual bowls and garnish with the crabmeat. Sprinkle with the chives and serve.

Avocados, 3, halved, pitted, peeled, and coarsely chopped

Serrano chiles, 2, seeded and chopped

Unsweetened coconut milk, 1 cup (8 fl oz/250 ml)

Lime juice, from 1 lime, or more to taste

Salt and white pepper

Lump crabmeat, ½ lb (250 g), picked over for shell fragments

Fresh chives, 2, snipped

SERVES 4

mexican-style pork & rice soup

Olive oil, 2 tablespoons

Boneless pork loin,
1 lb (500 g), cut into cubes

Yellow onion, 1 small, chopped

Garlic, 2 cloves, minced

Serrano chiles, 3, seeded and chopped

Long-grain rice, ¼ cup (2 oz/60 g)

Chicken broth, 5 cups (40 fl oz/1.25 l)

Fresh cilantro (fresh coriander), ¼ cup (⅓ oz/10 g) minced

Lime juice, from 1 lime

Salt and freshly ground pepper

SERVES 4–6

1 **Brown the pork**
In a large saucepan over medium-high heat, warm 1 tablespoon of the oil. When it is hot, working in batches if necessary to avoid crowding, add the pork and cook, turning as needed, until golden brown on all sides, about 6 minutes. Using a slotted spoon, transfer to a plate.

2 **Simmer the soup**
Reduce the heat to medium and add the remaining 1 tablespoon oil. Add the onion, garlic, chiles, and rice and stir to coat with the oil. Pour in the broth and bring to a boil. Reduce the heat to low, cover, and simmer until the rice is tender, about 15 minutes.

3 **Finish the soup**
Return the pork to the pan, stir in the cilantro and lime juice, and cook until the pork is cooked through, about 5 minutes. Season to taste with salt and pepper. Ladle into bowls and serve.

cook's tip

You can dress up this soup with
a colorful garnish of chopped
avocado and tomato. Serve with
warmed corn tortillas.

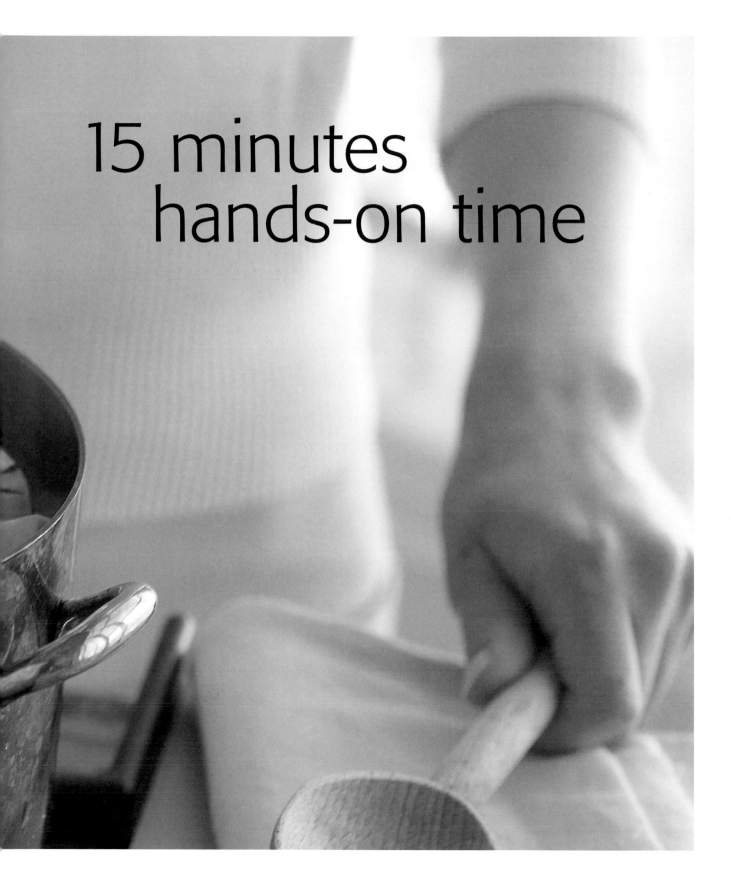

15 minutes
hands-on time

venetian rice & pea soup

Unsalted butter,
2 tablespoons

Shallot, 1, minced

Celery, 1 stalk, chopped

Short-grain white rice,
such as Arborio, ½ cup
(3½ oz/105 g)

Chicken broth, 3 cups
(24 fl oz/750 ml)

Frozen peas, 2 cups
(12 oz/375 g)

Parmesan cheese, ½ cup
(2 oz/60 g) freshly grated

Fresh flat-leaf (Italian)
parsley, 1 tablespoon minced

Salt and freshly ground
pepper

SERVES 4

1 Sauté the vegetables
In a large saucepan over medium heat, melt the butter.
Add the shallot and celery and sauté until the shallot is
translucent, about 2 minutes. Add the rice and cook, stirring,
until the grains are opaque, about 1 minute.

2 Cook the rice and peas
Raise the heat to medium-high, add the broth and
2 cups (16 fl oz/500 ml) water, and bring to a boil. Reduce the
heat to low, cover, and simmer until the rice is tender, about
15 minutes. Add the peas and cook, stirring occasionally, for
5 minutes longer. Just before serving, stir in the cheese and
parsley and season to taste with salt and pepper. Ladle into
bowls and serve.

cook's tip

You can substitute 2 lb (1 kg)
fresh English peas for the frozen
peas, adding them with the
broth and water. To shell the
peas, hold each pod over a bowl,
press your thumb against the
seam to split it, and then sweep
the peas into the bowl. This can
be done up to 1 day in advance;
store the peas in a resealable
plastic bag in the refrigerator.

cook's tip

To toast pecans, preheat the
oven to 325°F (165°C). Scatter
the pecans on a baking sheet
and toast, stirring occasionally,
until fragrant, about 10 minutes.
You can also toast them, shaking
often, in a dry frying pan over
medium heat for 10 minutes.

sweet potato soup

1 Sauté the vegetables

In a large saucepan over medium heat, melt the butter. Add the leek and celery and sauté until the leek is translucent, about 3 minutes. Add the sweet potatoes and broth, raise the heat to high, and bring to a boil. Reduce the heat to low, cover, and simmer until the sweet potatoes are tender, about 30 minutes.

2 Purée the soup

Using a food processor or blender, process the soup to a smooth purée. Return to the pan and reheat to serving temperature. Season to taste with salt and pepper. Ladle into bowls, garnish with the pecans, if using, and serve.

Unsalted butter,
1 tablespoon

Leek, 1, white part only, halved, rinsed, and thinly sliced

Celery, 2 stalks, chopped

Sweet potatoes, 2 large, peeled and cut into 2-inch (5-cm) pieces

Chicken or vegetable broth, 4 cups (32 fl oz/1 l)

Salt and freshly ground pepper

Pecans, ¼ cup (1 oz/30 g), toasted and chopped (optional)

SERVES 4

49

roasted
garlic soup

Garlic, 8 heads, top one-third
cut off

Olive oil, 4 tablespoons
(2 fl oz/60 ml)

Baguette, 8 slices

**Chicken or vegetable
broth,** 6 cups (48 fl oz/1.5 l)

**Salt and freshly ground
pepper**

SERVES 4

1 Roast the garlic
Preheat the oven to 325°F (165°C). Arrange the
garlic heads, cut side up, in a shallow baking dish. Drizzle with
2 tablespoons of the oil and cover the dish loosely with
aluminum foil. Roast until the cloves are very tender when
pierced with a fork, 1–1½ hours. When the heads are cool
enough to handle, squeeze the soft garlic pulp into a bowl.

2 Fry the bread
In a frying pan over medium-high heat, warm the
remaining 2 tablespoons oil. When it is hot, add the bread
slices, reduce the heat to medium, and fry the bread on each
side until golden, about 4 minutes total. Remove from the
heat and set aside.

3 Finish the soup
In a medium saucepan over medium-high heat,
combine the broth and garlic pulp, bring to a simmer, and
cook, stirring often, for 5 minutes. Using a food processor
or blender, process the soup to a smooth purée. Return
to the pan and reheat to serving temperature. Season to taste
with salt and pepper. Place 2 bread slices in each bowl, ladle
the soup over them, and serve.

cook's tip

For an easier version of this
soup, replace the fresh tomatoes
with 4 cups (32 fl oz/1 l) canned
fire-roasted tomatoes. Add to
the sautéed shallots along with
1 tablespoon of the basil in step
2, and sauté for 5 minutes before
adding the wine and water.

roasted tomato–basil soup

1 Roast the tomatoes

Preheat the oven to 400°F (200°C). Arrange the tomato halves, cut side up, in a large roasting pan. Sprinkle 1 tablespoon of the basil and the garlic evenly over the tomatoes. Drizzle 4 tablespoons of the oil evenly over the tomatoes. Roast until the tomatoes are soft when pierced with a fork and the skins slip off easily, about 40 minutes. Remove from the oven. Remove and discard the skins.

2 Simmer the soup

In a large saucepan over medium-high heat, warm the remaining 1 tablespoon oil. When it is hot, add the shallots and sauté until translucent, about 2 minutes. Add the roasted tomatoes and garlic, wine, and ½ cup (4 fl oz/125 ml) water and bring to a boil. Reduce the heat to medium-low and simmer, uncovered, until the tomatoes have broken down, the mixture has thickened, and the flavors have blended, about 20 minutes. Season to taste with salt and pepper.

3 Purée the soup

Using a food processor or blender, purée the soup, stopping while it is still coarse if you like a rustic soup, and continuing until smooth if you want a more refined soup. Return to the pan and reheat to serving temperature. Ladle the soup into bowls, garnish with the remaining basil, and serve.

Plum (Roma) tomatoes, 10, halved lengthwise

Fresh basil, 4 tablespoons chopped

Garlic, 2 cloves, minced

Olive oil, 5 tablespoons (2½ fl oz/75 ml)

Shallots, 4, halved

Dry white wine, 1½ cups (12 fl oz/375 ml)

Salt and freshly ground pepper

SERVES 4

north african chickpea soup

Olive oil, 2 tablespoons, plus more for drizzling

Carrot, 1, finely chopped

Yellow onion, ¼, finely chopped

Tomato, 1, finely chopped

Red bell pepper (capsicum), 1 small, seeded and finely chopped

Salt and freshly ground black pepper

Ground cumin, ½ teaspoon

Ground turmeric, ¼ teaspoon

Cayenne pepper, ½ teaspoon

Chickpeas (garbanzo beans), 2 cans (14½ oz/ 455 g each), drained and rinsed

Zucchini (courgettes), 2 small, chopped

Chicken broth, 5 cups (40 fl oz/1.25 l)

SERVES 4

1 Sauté the vegetables

In a large saucepan over medium heat, warm the 2 tablespoons oil. When it is hot, add the carrot and onion and sauté until slightly softened, about 3 minutes. Add the tomato, bell pepper, 1 teaspoon salt, cumin, turmeric, and cayenne. Sauté until fragrant, about 1 minute.

2 Finish the soup

Add the chickpeas, zucchini, and broth. Raise the heat to medium-high and bring to a boil. Reduce the heat to medium-low and simmer, uncovered, until the zucchini is tender and the flavors are blended, about 15 minutes. Season to taste with salt and black pepper. Ladle into bowls, drizzle with olive oil, and serve.

cook's tip

In place of the fresh turkey
breast, use a purchased rotisserie
chicken. Remove and discard
the skin and bones, and cut the
meat into bite-sized pieces.
Add to the soup along with the
yogurt in step 2.

turkey
mulligatawny soup

1 Sauté the turkey and vegetables

In a large stockpot or Dutch oven over medium heat, melt the butter. Add the turkey and sauté until lightly browned on all sides, about 7 minutes. Using a slotted spoon, transfer to a plate and set aside. Add the onion, celery, carrots, and garlic to the pot and sauté until the onion is translucent, about 7 minutes. Stir in the curry powder and cook, stirring, for 2–3 minutes longer to blend the flavors.

2 Simmer the soup

Add the broth and browned turkey to the vegetables in the pot and bring just to a simmer over high heat. Reduce the heat to medium, add the rice, and cook, uncovered, until the rice is tender and the turkey is cooked through, 15–20 minutes. Stir in the yogurt and simmer over medium heat for 10 minutes to blend the flavors. Season to taste with salt and pepper. Ladle the soup into bowls, garnish with the cilantro, if using, and serve.

Unsalted butter, 3 tablespoons

Boneless, skinless turkey breast, 1 half, about 1 1/2 lb (750 g), cut into bite-sized cubes

Yellow onion, 1, finely chopped

Celery, 3 stalks, finely chopped

Carrots, 2, finely chopped

Garlic, 1 clove, minced

Curry powder, 1 tablespoon

Chicken broth, 4 cups (32 fl oz/1 l)

Long-grain white rice, 1/2 cup (3 1/2 oz/105 g)

Plain yogurt, 1 cup (8 oz/250 g)

Salt and freshly ground pepper

Fresh cilantro (fresh coriander), 1/4 cup (1/3 oz/ 10 g) minced (optional)

SERVES 4

roasted root vegetable soup

Celery root (celeriac),
1 large or 2 small, peeled and cut into slices 1 inch (2.5 cm) thick

Parsnips, 2, peeled and quartered lengthwise

Leeks, 2 large, white part only, halved and rinsed

Garlic, 1 head, top one-third cut off

Olive oil, ¼ cup (2 fl oz/ 60 ml)

Herbes de Provence,
1 teaspoon

Salt and freshly ground pepper

Vermouth or brandy,
1 teaspoon

Half-and-half (half cream),
2½ cups (20 fl oz/625 ml)

Chicken broth, 3 cups
(24 fl oz/750 ml)

SERVES 4

1 **Roast the vegetables**
Preheat the oven to 325°F (165°C). Arrange the celery root, parsnips, leeks (cut side down), and garlic (cut side up) in a single layer on a baking sheet. Sprinkle with the olive oil, herbes de Provence, and a little salt and pepper. Roast for 45 minutes. Turn the garlic and the vegetables, cover the pan loosely with aluminum foil, and continue to roast until the vegetables are tender, about 45 minutes longer.

2 **Purée the soup**
Squeeze the pulp from the garlic into a food processor or blender, discarding the skins. Add the rest of the roasted vegetables in batches and process to a coarse purée. Transfer to a large saucepan over medium-high heat. Add the vermouth, half-and-half, and broth, stir well, and bring to a boil. Reduce the heat to low, cover, and simmer for 10–15 minutes to blend the flavors. Season to taste with salt and pepper. Ladle the soup into bowls and serve.

cook's tip

If you can't find celery root, use ¾ lb (375 g) russet potatoes, peeled and sliced, and 1–2 celery stalks, cut into 2-inch (5-cm) pieces. Arrange on the baking sheet with the other vegetables and roast as directed.

cook's tip

An ancient Incan grain, quinoa
(pronounced KEEN-wah) is rich
in protein. Other nutty grains,
such as pearl barley or farro, can
be substituted for the quinoa.

mushroom-quinoa soup

1 Make the roux
In a large saucepan over medium heat, melt the butter. Remove from the heat and slowly add the flour, whisking out any lumps. Add ½ teaspoon salt and ¼ teaspoon pepper. Return the pan to medium heat and cook the roux, stirring constantly, until it begins to brown, about 3 minutes. Add the leek, carrot, and celery and stir. Slowly add the wine while whisking constantly. Reduce the heat to low and let simmer, stirring occasionally, until the flavors have blended and the roux has thickened, about 20 minutes.

2 Cook the mushrooms and quinoa
Meanwhile, in another saucepan over medium heat, bring the broth to a simmer. Add the mushrooms and cook, uncovered, for 10 minutes. When the roux mixture is ready, add the broth and mushrooms and stir well. Bring to a boil, then reduce the heat to medium-low. Add the quinoa and simmer, uncovered, until tender, about 20 minutes. Season to taste with salt and pepper. Ladle into bowls and serve.

Unsalted butter, 2 tablespoons

Flour, 2 tablespoons

Salt and freshly ground pepper

Leek, 1, white part only, halved, rinsed, and thinly sliced

Carrot, 1, finely chopped

Celery, 1 stalk, finely chopped

Dry red wine, 1 cup (8 fl oz/ 250 ml)

Vegetable or chicken broth, 4 cups (32 fl oz/1 l)

Cremini mushrooms, 1 lb (500 g), stems removed and caps quartered

Quinoa, ⅓ cup (2 oz/60 g), well rinsed

SERVES 4

mexican meatball soup

Zucchini (courgettes),
2, coarsely chopped

Celery, 3 stalks, coarsely
chopped

Beef broth, 2½ cups
(20 fl oz/625 ml)

**Whole plum (Roma)
tomatoes,** 1 can (14½ oz/
455 g), coarsely chopped,
with juice

Tomato paste, 2 tablespoons

Yellow onion, 1, chopped

Fresh oregano,
4½ teaspoons minced

Chili powder, 1 teaspoon

**Salt and freshly ground
pepper**

Ground (minced) beef,
1 lb (500 g)

Egg, 1, lightly beaten

Fresh bread crumbs,
¼ cup (½ oz/15 g)

SERVES 4

1 **Make the soup base**
In a large saucepan over medium heat, combine the zucchini, celery, broth, tomatoes and juice, tomato paste, all but 2 tablespoons of the onion, ½ teaspoon of the oregano, the chili powder, and 1 cup (8 fl oz/250 ml) water. Bring to a boil, reduce the heat to low, and simmer, uncovered, until the vegetables are soft and the flavors are blended, about 30 minutes. Season to taste with salt.

2 **Prepare the meatballs**
Meanwhile, in a bowl, combine the ground beef, egg, bread crumbs, remaining onion and oregano, 1½ teaspoons salt, and 1 teaspoon pepper. Mix gently with your hands, then shape into balls about 1 inch (2.5 cm) in diameter; set aside.

3 **Finish the soup**
When the soup base is ready, using a large spoon, gently slide the meatballs into the simmering broth. Cook until opaque throughout, 7–9 minutes. Ladle the soup into individual bowls and serve.

cook's tip

You can prepare the meatballs
in advance and freeze them
in an airtight container for up to
3 months. To use, defrost in the
refrigerator overnight. Add to
the soup as directed in step 3.

cook's tip

The beets can be roasted up to
2 days in advance. Trim and peel
them, then store in an airtight
container in the refrigerator until
needed. You can also roast
additional beets at the same time,
to be sliced and used in salads.

roasted
beet soup

1 Roast the beets

Preheat the oven to 350°F (180°C). Put the beets in a baking dish and drizzle with the oil, turning them to coat well. Roast until the beets are easily pierced with a fork, about 1 hour. Remove from the oven. When the beets are cool enough to handle, peel and coarsely chop them.

2 Cook the soup

In a large saucepan over medium heat, melt the butter. Add the onion and sauté until translucent, about 2 minutes. Add the chopped beets and the broth, bring to a simmer, reduce the heat to low, and cook, uncovered, for about 10 minutes to blend the flavors.

3 Purée the soup

Using a food processor or blender, process the soup to a smooth purée. Serve warm or, for a chilled soup, let cool to room temperature, transfer to an airtight container, and refrigerate for 2–8 hours or for up to 24 hours. Adjust the seasoning with salt and pepper. Ladle into bowls, garnish with the cheese and dill, and serve.

Red or yellow beets, 3 large, trimmed, leaving 1 inch (2.5 cm) of stem

Olive oil, 1 ½ tablespoons

Unsalted butter, 1 tablespoon

Yellow onion, ¼, chopped

Chicken, beef, or vegetable broth, 4 cups (32 fl oz/1 l)

Salt and freshly ground pepper

Feta cheese, ½ cup (2 ½ oz/75 g) crumbled

Fresh dill, 2 tablespoons coarsely chopped

SERVES 4

vietnamese beef noodle soup

Eye of round beef steak, ½ lb (250 g), cut across the grain into slices ⅛ inch (3 mm) thick

Canola oil, 2 tablespoons

Asian fish sauce, 3½ teaspoons

Salt

Beef broth, 6 cups (48 fl oz/ 1.5 l)

Fresh ginger, 3-inch (7.5-cm) piece, thinly sliced

Coriander seeds, 1 teaspoon

Cinnamon stick, ½-inch (12-mm) piece

Rice vermicelli, 8–10 oz (250–315 g)

Bean sprouts, ¼ lb (125 g)

Fresh basil, preferably Thai, ½ cup (¾ oz/20 g) coarsely chopped

Limes, 2, quartered

SERVES 4

1 **Marinate the beef**
In a resealable plastic bag, combine the beef slices, 1 tablespoon of the oil, 1½ teaspoons of the fish sauce, and ¼ teaspoon salt. Seal the bag and massage with your hands to distribute the marinade evenly. Set aside for 15 minutes at room temperature or for up to overnight in the refrigerator.

2 **Cook the noodles**
In a large saucepan over medium-high heat, combine the beef broth, ginger, coriander seeds, cinnamon stick, and the remaining 2 teaspoons fish sauce and bring to a boil. Reduce the heat to low, cover, and simmer for 30 minutes. Meanwhile, bring a large pot of water to a boil, add the rice vermicelli, and cook just until tender, according to the package directions. Drain, rinse under running cold water, and divide evenly among bowls.

3 **Finish the soup**
In a frying pan over high heat, warm the remaining 1 tablespoon oil. When it is hot, add the beef and cook, stirring often, until seared on both sides, about 4 minutes total. Remove from the pan and set aside. Strain the broth through a fine-mesh sieve, return to the saucepan, and bring to a boil over medium-high heat. Add the bean sprouts, basil, and beef and cook just until the bean sprouts begin to wilt, about 3 minutes. Ladle over the vermicelli and serve. Pass the lime wedges at the table to squeeze over the soup.

cook's tip

To make the meat easier to slice
thinly, first place it in the freezer
for about 30 minutes, then slice
it against the grain with a very
sharp knife.

cook's tip

For a lighter soup, omit the 4 cups
milk and 1 cup cream. Replace
them with 5 cups (40 fl oz/1.25 l)
good-quality chicken broth.

spicy corn soup

1 Cook the bacon

In a large saucepan over medium heat, cook the bacon, stirring occasionally, until it begins to crisp, about 5 minutes. Transfer the bacon to paper towels to drain. Add the onion, celery, chile, and garlic to the bacon drippings and sauté just until lightly browned, 6–7 minutes.

2 Simmer the soup

Raise the heat to medium-high, add the milk, cream, and potatoes, and bring to a boil. Reduce the heat to low and simmer, uncovered, until the potatoes are tender, about 15 minutes. Stir in the corn and red pepper flakes and simmer until the corn is tender, about 5 minutes.

3 Purée the soup

Transfer about 2 cups (16 fl oz/500 ml) of the solids to a blender or food processor and process to a smooth purée. Return to the pan and reheat to serving temperature. Season to taste with salt and black pepper. Ladle into bowls, garnish with the bacon, and serve.

Bacon, 3 slices, chopped

Yellow onion, 1 small, chopped

Celery, 1 stalk, chopped

Poblano chile, 1, seeded and chopped

Garlic, 2 cloves, minced

Milk, 4 cups (32 fl oz/1 l)

Heavy (double) cream, 1 cup (8 fl oz/250 ml)

Boiling potatoes, 2, peeled and cut into bite-sized cubes

Corn kernels, 3 cups (18 oz/560 g), fresh or frozen

Red pepper flakes, ½ teaspoon

Salt and freshly ground black pepper

SERVES 4

ratatouille soup

Olive oil, 3 tablespoons

Garlic, 2 cloves, minced

Eggplant (aubergine),
1, peeled and cut into small
cubes

Zucchini (courgette),
1, chopped

Yellow onion, 1, quartered

**Red bell pepper
(capsicum),** 1, seeded
and chopped

Tomatoes, 4 large, peeled
and quartered

Chicken broth, 2–3 cups
(16–24 fl oz/500–750 ml)

**Salt and freshly ground
pepper**

Fresh basil, 4 tablespoons
minced

SERVES 4

1 Cook the vegetables
In a saucepan over medium heat, warm 2 tablespoons
of the oil. When the oil is hot, add the garlic and sauté until
fragrant, about 1 minute. Add the eggplant, zucchini, onion,
and bell pepper and cook, stirring occasionally, until the
vegetables have softened slightly, 10–15 minutes. Add the
tomatoes and the remaining 1 tablespoon oil. Cook, stirring
occasionally, until the tomatoes begin to break down, about
15 minutes. Reduce the heat to low and simmer until the
flavors have blended, about 15 minutes longer.

2 Purée the vegetables
Add 1 cup (8 oz/250 ml) of the broth to the vegetables.
Using a blender or food processor, process the vegetables to
a smooth purée. Return to the pan and place over medium heat.
Add enough additional broth to make a thick soup. Simmer
until heated through, about 5 minutes. Season to taste with salt
and pepper. Ladle into bowls, garnish with the basil, and serve.

cook's tip

For a classic ratatouille, do not
purée the soup and leave out
the chicken broth. Add 1 cup
(7 oz/220 g) tomato purée with
the fresh tomatoes. This versatile
Provençal stew can be used as
a base for sausages, pan-seared
fish, or tossed with pasta.

make more
to store

bok choy & shiitake soup

VEGETABLE STOCK

Leeks, 5 large

Yellow onions, 5, quartered

Carrots, 8, coarsely chopped

Celery, 6 stalks, coarsely chopped

Fresh flat-leaf (Italian) parsley, 6 sprigs

Button mushrooms, ½ lb (250 g), halved

Peppercorns, 10

Salt

Bok choy, 1 head, halved lengthwise and thinly sliced

Shiitake mushrooms, ½ lb (250 g), thinly sliced

Green (spring) onions, 4, including green tops, sliced

Snow peas (mangetouts), ¼ lb (125 g), thinly sliced

Soy sauce, 2 teaspoons

Asian sesame oil, ¼ teaspoon

SERVES 4

makes about 5 qt (5 l) stock total

This versatile stock serves as the building block for many favorite soups, including this one featuring Asian ingredients. This recipe yields enough stock for the bok choy and shiitake soup, plus four others.

1 Make the vegetable stock
Trim, halve, and rinse the leeks, then cut into chunks. In a stockpot, combine the leeks, onions, carrots, celery, parsley, button mushrooms, and peppercorns. Add 5 qt (5 l) water and bring to a boil over high heat. Reduce the heat to medium-low, cover partially, and simmer until the vegetables are very soft and the flavors have blended, about 1 hour. Season to taste with salt. Pour the contents of the stockpot through a fine-mesh sieve into a large bowl. Press down on the solids to extract all the flavor, and discard the solids.

2 Simmer the soup
In a large saucepan over medium-high heat, bring 4 cups (32 fl oz/1 l) of the vegetable stock to a simmer. Add the bok choy, shiitake mushrooms, green onions, snow peas, soy sauce, and sesame oil. Reduce the heat to medium-low and simmer, uncovered, until the vegetables are tender, about 10 minutes. Season to taste with salt and pepper. Ladle into bowls and serve.

storage tip

Stock will keep in an airtight container in the refrigerator for up to 3 days or in the freezer for up to 3 months. For ease of use, you can store the stock in 1-cup (8–fl oz/250-ml) or 1-qt (1-l) plastic containers, ice cube trays, or heavy-duty resealable bags of various sizes.

cook's tip

To remove the tough ends from
asparagus, hold each spear
at either end and bend until it
snaps. Discard the woody base.

creamy
asparagus soup

1 Simmer the asparagus
In a large saucepan over medium heat, melt the butter. Add the shallot and sauté until translucent, about 1 minute. Add the stock, wine, and asparagus, raise the heat to medium-high, and bring to a boil. Reduce the heat to low and simmer, uncovered, until the asparagus is tender, about 10 minutes.

2 Purée the soup
Using a food processor or blender, process the soup to a smooth purée. Return the soup to the pan and place over low heat. Stir in the cream and season to taste with salt and pepper. Reheat to serving temperature. Ladle the soup into bowls, garnish with the tarragon, and serve.

Vegetable Stock, 4 cups (32 fl oz/1 l), homemade (page 74) or purchased

Unsalted butter, 2 tablespoons

Shallot, 1, minced

Dry white wine, ½ cup (4 fl oz/125 ml)

Asparagus, 1½ lb (750 g), tough ends removed, cut into 1-inch (2.5-cm) pieces

Heavy (double) cream, ¼ cup (2 fl oz/60 ml)

Salt and freshly ground pepper

Fresh tarragon, 2 tablespoons chopped

SERVES 4

spring vegetable soup

Vegetable Stock, 4 cups (32 fl oz/1 l), homemade (page 74) or purchased

Sugar snap peas, 1 lb (500 g), trimmed and coarsely chopped

Leek, 1, white part only, halved, rinsed, and thinly sliced

Green (spring) onions, 3, white part only, chopped

Salt and freshly ground pepper

Fresh flat-leaf (Italian) parsley, 2 tablespoons minced

Fresh chives, 2 tablespoons minced

Lemon, 1, quartered

SERVES 4

1 Simmer the vegetables

In a saucepan over medium-high heat, bring the stock to a boil. Add the sugar snap peas, leek, and green onions, reduce the heat to low, cover, and simmer until the sugar snap peas are just tender, 10–15 minutes.

2 Purée the soup

Using a food processor or blender, process the soup to a coarse purée. Return to the pan and reheat to serving temperature. Season to taste with salt and pepper. Ladle the soup into bowls, garnish with the parsley and chives, and serve. Pass the lemon wedges at the table to squeeze over the soup.

cook's tip

Instead of sugar snap peas,
you can use 1 lb (500 g) freshly
shelled English peas or 1 lb
(500 g) sliced asparagus. They
will take 15–25 minutes to cook,
depending on their maturity.

chicken soup with kale

CHICKEN STOCK

Whole chicken, 1, about 3½ lb (1.75 kg), quartered

Yellow onions, 2, quartered

Leeks, 2 small, white and pale green parts, halved, rinsed, and coarsely chopped

Celery, 4 stalks, quartered

Carrots, 4, quartered

Fresh flat-leaf (Italian) parsley, 6 sprigs

Fresh thyme, 6 sprigs

Peppercorns, 10

Salt and freshly ground pepper

Russet potatoes, 2, peeled and cut into cubes

Kale, ½ bunch, stems removed and leaves chopped

Lemon juice, 1 tablespoon

Salt and freshly ground pepper

SERVES 4

makes about 4½ qt (4.5 l) stock total

A full-bodied chicken stock is indispensable for making soup. This version yields both enough stock and enough meat for this simple soup as well as two more recipes on the following pages.

1 Simmer the stock

Put the chicken in a stockpot. Add water to cover by 1½ inches (4 cm). Bring to a simmer over medium-high heat and skim any foam from the surface. Add the onions, leeks, celery, carrots, parsley, thyme, peppercorns, and 2 teaspoons salt. Return to a boil. Reduce the heat to low and simmer gently, uncovered, until the chicken is cooked through, about 1 hour.

2 Reserve the chicken

Transfer the chicken to a platter, let cool slightly, then remove the meat, reserving the skin and bones. Reserve 2 cups (12 oz/375 g) of the meat and refrigerate the rest for another recipe. Return the skin and bones to the pot and continue to simmer, uncovered, for 1 hour. Pour the contents of the pot through a fine-mesh sieve into a large bowl, press down on the solids to extract the flavor, and discard the solids.

3 Finish the soup

In a saucepan over medium-high heat, combine 6 cups (48 fl oz/1.5 l) stock and the potatoes and bring to a boil. Reduce the heat to low and simmer, uncovered, until the potatoes are tender, about 10 minutes. Add the kale and simmer for 10 minutes. Add the reserved chicken and heat through, 2 minutes. Add the lemon juice and season to taste with salt and pepper. Ladle the soup into bowls and serve.

storage tip

To store the stock, let it cool
completely, cover, and refrigerate
for several hours or overnight.
Before using the stock, skim the
fat from the surface. The stock
will keep in airtight containers
in the refrigerator for up to
3 days or in the freezer for up
to 3 months. The chicken meat
will keep in the refrigerator
for up to 3 days.

cook's tip

To make chicken and rice soup,
substitute 1 cup (5 oz/155 g)
cooked white rice for the noodles.
Add the rice to the soup about
2 minutes before serving in step 2.

chicken noodle soup

1 Prepare the soup

In a large saucepan over medium heat, warm the oil. When it is hot, add the celery, leek, and carrot and sauté until softened, about 5 minutes. Pour in the stock and add the bay leaf, thyme, and shredded chicken. Bring to a boil over medium-high heat. Add the noodles, stir well, and cook just until the noodles are tender, about 10 minutes.

2 Season the soup

Remove and discard the bay leaf from the soup. Season to taste with salt and pepper. Ladle into bowls, garnish with the parsley, and serve.

Chicken Stock, 5 cups (40 fl oz/1.25 l), homemade (page 80) or purchased

Cooked shredded chicken, 2 cups (12 oz/375 g), homemade (page 80) or purchased

Olive oil, 2 tablespoons

Celery, 2 stalks, finely chopped

Leek, 1, white part only, halved, rinsed, and thinly sliced

Carrot, 1, finely chopped

Bay leaf, 1

Dried thyme, 1/4 teaspoon

Dried egg noodles, 1/2 lb (250 g)

Salt and freshly ground pepper

Fresh flat-leaf (Italian) parsley, 1/4 cup (1/3 oz/10 g) minced

SERVES 4

chicken-tortilla soup

Chicken Stock, 6 cups (48 fl oz/1.5 l), homemade (page 80) or purchased

Cooked shredded chicken, 2 cups (12 oz/375 g), homemade (page 80) or purchased

Olive oil, 1 tablespoon

White onion, ½, finely chopped

Chili powder, 2 teaspoons

Lime juice, from 3–4 limes

Salt

Corn tortilla chips, 1½ cups (4 oz/125 g), broken into pieces

Queso fresco, ½ cup (2½ oz/75 g) crumbled, or Monterey jack cheese, ½ cup (2 oz/60 g) shredded

Avocado, 1, halved, pitted, peeled, and cubed

Fresh cilantro (fresh coriander), ¼ cup (⅓ oz/10 g) chopped

SERVES 4–6

1 Sauté the onion

In a large saucepan over medium-high heat, warm the oil. When it is hot, add the onion and sauté until translucent, about 3 minutes. Add the chili powder and stir until fragrant, about 1 minute. Pour in the stock and bring to a boil.

2 Finish the soup

Add the shredded chicken, reduce the heat to medium, and simmer until the chicken is heated through, about 3 minutes. Add the lime juice and salt to taste. Ladle into bowls, garnish with the tortilla chips, *queso fresco,* avocado, and cilantro, and serve.

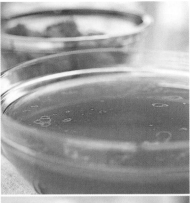

cook's tip

If you do not have shredded
chicken on hand, purchase
a rotisserie chicken and shred the
breast meat for use in this soup.
Reserve the remaining meat
for another use. Alternatively,
poach or bake a whole, skinless,
boneless chicken breast. Let
cool, then shred the meat.

cook's tip

For an almost instant soup, use
canned lentils instead of dried.
Add to the soup in step 2 and
cook for 5 minutes before adding
the spinach. Canned lentils
are available at well-stocked
supermarkets.

lentil & spinach soup

1 Sauté the bacon and vegetables
In a large saucepan over medium heat, sauté the bacon until the fat is rendered, about 5 minutes. Add the carrot and onion and cook until the onion is translucent, about 2 minutes. Add the garlic, thyme, and 1 teaspoon salt and sauté until the garlic is soft, about 1 minute. Stir in the lentils.

2 Simmer the lentils
Add the stock, tomato paste, and 1 cup (8 fl oz/ 250 ml) water, raise the heat to high, and bring to a boil. Reduce the heat to low, cover partially, and simmer until the lentils are tender to the bite, 25–30 minutes. Add the spinach and simmer until wilted, about 2 minutes longer.

3 Season the soup
Season the soup to taste with salt and pepper. Ladle into bowls and serve.

Chicken Stock, 4 cups (32 fl oz/1 l), homemade (page 80) or purchased

Bacon, 3 slices, chopped

Carrot, 1/2, finely chopped

Yellow onion, 1/2 small, finely chopped

Garlic, 2 cloves, minced

Fresh thyme, 1 teaspoon minced

Salt and freshly ground pepper

Dried lentils, 1 cup (7 oz/ 220 g), picked over and rinsed

Tomato paste, 2 tablespoons

Baby spinach, 3 cups (3 oz/90 g), chopped

SERVES 4

tortellini in broth

BEEF STOCK

Beef and veal soup bones, 6 lb (3 kg)

Carrots, 3, cut into slices ½ inch (12 mm) thick

Yellow onions, 3, cut into slices ½ inch (12 mm) thick

Salt and freshly ground pepper

Celery, 3 stalks, coarsely chopped

Leeks, 2, white and pale green parts, halved, rinsed, and coarsely chopped

Garlic, 1 clove

Cheese tortellini, 12 oz (375 g)

Parmesan cheese, ⅓ cup (1½ oz/45 g) freshly grated

Fresh basil, ¼ cup (⅓ oz/ 10 g) slivered

SERVES 4

makes about 5 qt (5 l) stock total

The beef stock in this classic Italian dish needs a lot of time to simmer, but the flavorful result is worth the effort. This recipe makes enough stock for the tortellini soup plus the following two recipes.

1 Roast the bones
Preheat the oven to 400°F (200°C). Arrange the bones in a single layer in a roasting pan. Add the carrot and onion slices. Roast until the bones are browned, 45–60 minutes. Transfer the bones and vegetables to a stockpot or Dutch oven.

2 Simmer the stock
Add 8 qt (8 l) water, 1 tablespoon salt, and 2 teaspoons pepper to the stockpot. Bring to a boil over medium heat. Using a slotted spoon, skim off any foam from the surface and then add the celery, leeks, and garlic. Reduce the heat to low, cover partially, and simmer for 4–5 hours, skimming any foam from the surface. Remove the bones from the pot and discard. Pour the contents of the pot through a fine-mesh sieve into a large bowl and discard the solids.

3 Cook the tortellini
In a saucepan over medium-high heat, bring 6 cups (48 fl oz/1.5 l) stock to a boil. Add the tortellini and cook for about 5 minutes, or according to the package directions. Season to taste with salt and pepper. Ladle the tortellini and stock into bowls, garnish with the cheese and basil, and serve.

storage tip

Let the stock cool completely.
Cover and refrigerate for several
hours or overnight. Before using
the stock, lift off and discard the
fat on the surface. The stock will
keep in airtight containers in the
refrigerator for up to 3 days or
in the freezer for up to 3 months.

cook's tip

For an earthier soup, replace
the button mushrooms with
a variety of wild and cultivated
mushrooms, such as cremini,
chanterelle, shiitake, or porcini
(ceps) mushrooms.

beef & barley soup

1 Cook the barley
In a saucepan over medium-high heat, bring 3 cups (24 fl oz/750 ml) water to a boil. Add 1 teaspoon salt and the barley and return to a boil. Reduce the heat to low, cover, and cook the barley until just tender, about 1½ hours. Drain and set aside.

2 Prepare the soup base
While the barley is cooking, in a large saucepan over medium heat, melt the butter. Add the onion and mushrooms and sauté until the onion is translucent and the mushrooms have released their juices, about 5 minutes. Add the stock and beef, reduce the heat to low, and simmer, uncovered, for about 10 minutes.

3 Finish the soup
When the barley is ready, add it to the soup and simmer over medium heat for 5 minutes to blend the flavors. Season to taste with salt and pepper. Ladle into bowls and serve.

Beef Stock, 4 cups (32 fl oz/ 1 l), homemade (page 88) or purchased

Salt and freshly ground pepper

Pearl barley, ¼ cup (2 oz/60 g)

Unsalted butter, 2 tablespoons

Yellow onion, 1 small, chopped

Button mushrooms, ½ lb (250 g), finely chopped

Boneless beef sirloin, ½ lb (250 g), cut into thin slices and then finely chopped

SERVES 4

french onion soup

Beef Stock, 2 qt (2 l), homemade (page 88) or purchased

Unsalted butter, 4 tablespoons (2 oz/60 g)

Olive oil, 4 tablespoons (2 fl oz/60 ml)

Yellow onions, 2 lb (1 kg), thinly sliced

Sugar, ½ teaspoon

Salt and freshly ground pepper

Flour, 1½ tablespoons

Dry white wine, ½ cup (4 fl oz/125 ml)

French bread, 12–16 slices, each ½ inch (12 mm) thick

Garlic, 3 cloves, halved

Gruyère cheese, ½ lb (250 g), shredded

SERVES 6–8

1 Caramelize the onions

In a large frying pan or Dutch oven over medium heat, melt the butter with 1 tablespoon of the oil. Add the onions and cook, stirring occasionally, until golden, 4–5 minutes. Reduce the heat to low, cover, and cook, stirring occasionally, for 15 minutes. Uncover, add the sugar and ½ teaspoon salt, and cook, stirring occasionally, until the onions are caramelized, about 25 minutes. Add the flour and stir for 2–3 minutes.

2 Simmer the soup

In another saucepan, bring the stock and wine to a boil over high heat. Slowly add to the onions, stirring to blend. Add 1 teaspoon pepper. Reduce the heat to medium, cover partially, and simmer until the onions begin to break down and melt into the stock, about 45 minutes.

3 Finish the soup

Meanwhile, preheat the broiler. Place the bread on a baking sheet, drizzle with the remaining olive oil, and toast under the broiler, turning once, until golden, 3–4 minutes on each side. Rub the bread with the cut sides of the garlic and set aside. Reduce the oven temperature to 400°F (200°C). Place 6–8 ovenproof bowls on a baking sheet. Ladle the soup into the bowls, filling them about three-fourths full. Top each serving with 2 slices of toast. Sprinkle with the cheese. Bake until the cheese is golden brown, about 15 minutes. Remove from the oven and serve.

cook's tip

The onions can be caramelized
a day ahead. Let cool to room
temperature and then store,
covered, in the refrigerator until
you are ready to finish the soup.

the smarter cook

Even the heartiest soups don't have to involve a lot of work. Most of the recipes in this book require less than 30 minutes to prepare. All of them reflect smart cooking, which calls for mastering a few key strategies: stocking your pantry, putting together a weekly meal plan, and cooking a double batch of soup when you have a little time. By planning ahead, you'll be able to put delicious homemade soups on the table in record time any night of the week.

Keep your pantry stocked and you'll always have the basic ingredients for a quick supper. Plan your meals and you'll make fewer trips to the store. Cook up a big batch of stock to use in multiple recipes and you'll have a head start. In the following pages, you'll find tips on how to manage your time and stock your kitchen–the keys to becoming a smarter cook.

get started

The keys to smarter cooking are planning and organization. This means not only keeping your pantry and refrigerator stocked with basic soup-making ingredients (pages 104–107), but also giving some thought to how cooking fits into your schedule. It's a good idea to draw up a weekly meal plan, too, a task made simple with this collection of quick and easy recipes.

plan a meal around soup

Getting into the habit of making a weekly meal plan can save you hours of shopping and kitchen time. It takes the worry out of figuring out what to feed your family and helps provide make-ahead opportunities that will save you time later. Once you have mapped out your meals, you can draw up a list of the fresh ingredients you need to make the recipes. You can pick these up in just a few efficient shopping trips.

■ **Soup is the perfect anchor for a meal.** Soup is flavorful, filling, and easy to cook, serve, store, and reheat. And whether light and meatless or hearty and substantial, soup can be a healthful mainstay and an inexpensive dinnertime solution. Use this book to build a repertoire of reliable soups that you and your family enjoy, and plan to serve at least one or two soup meals a week.

■ **Soup can be a first course or a main course.** Serve a lighter soup, such as Cucumber Soup (page 34), as a first course before a meat or fish main course. Or, offer a heartier soup, such as Beef & Barley Soup (page 91), as the centerpiece of the meal, accompanying it with a salad of mixed greens or a dish of simple steamed or roasted vegetables.

■ **Soup is best when made from seasonal ingredients.** Choose soups that take advantage of the best fresh ingredients of the season (see Think Seasonally, page 99). You'll enjoy better flavors, and you'll probably save money, too, because ingredients in season are often less expensive. Pick recipes that fit the weather: hearty, warming soups in autumn and winter, lighter fare and chilled soups in spring and summer. Be flexible once you're at the market to take advantage of the freshest ingredients.

ROUND IT OUT

bread Warm crusty artisanal bread and serve with extra-virgin olive oil, or warm wedges of purchased corn bread and serve with butter. Spread toasted bread slices with Dijon mustard, top with grated cheese, and melt under the broiler (grill), or top toasted baguette slices with purchased spreads such as tapenade, hummus, or pâté for crostini.

salad Choose salad ingredients that complement the soup you are serving, such as pairing a green salad with pears and walnuts with autumnal Sweet Potato Soup (page 49), or Caesar salad with Roasted Tomato–Basil Soup (page 53).

vegetables Serve steamed, sautéed, or roasted seasonal vegetables, such as roasted asparagus dressed with olive oil and shaved Parmesan cheese.

tomatoes Slice ripe tomatoes, arrange on a plate, and season with olive oil, salt, and pepper. Top with crumbled feta cheese, olives, or chopped fresh herbs.

sliced meats Assemble a platter of salami, prosciutto, or smoked turkey.

cheeses Set out two or three good-quality cheeses, including a soft, creamy type and a harder slicing cheese.

sample meals

IN MINUTES meals include soups and accompaniments that can be put together quickly. FROM THE PANTRY meals maximize ingredients from your pantry, saving you a trip to the store. FIT FOR COMPANY meals include ideas for stress-free get-togethers, complete with a wine suggestion.

IN MINUTES	FROM THE PANTRY	FIT FOR COMPANY
Creamy Spinach Soup (page 10) Rotisserie chicken	**Potato Cheddar Soup** (page 25) Mixed salad greens with balsamic vinaigrette	**Florentine White Bean Soup** (page 26) Braised sausages & greens *Chianti*
Clam Chowder (page 17) Mixed salad greens with balsamic vinaigrette	**Cucumber Soup** (page 34) Smoked salmon Toasted baguette slices	**Thai Chicken-Coconut Soup** (page 30) Sliced cucumber & red onion salad with rice vinegar dressing *Dry Riesling*
Cauliflower Soup (page 18) Broiled (grilled) chicken sausages & zucchini (courgettes)	**Curried Carrot Soup** (page 38) Toasted pita wedges with hummus	**Crab & Avocado Soup** (page 41) Butter lettuce, fennel & orange segments with citrus vinaigrette *Sauvignon Blanc*
Cajun Shrimp Soup (page 33) Steamed white rice Sautéed okra	**Roasted Garlic Soup** (page 50) Sliced ripe tomatoes with olive oil & crumbled feta	**Venetian Rice & Pea Soup** (page 46) Grilled flank steak with black pepper Arugula (rocket) & Parmesan salad with balsamic vinaigrette *Cabernet Sauvignon*
Spicy Gazpacho (page 37) Mixed salad greens with citrus vinaigrette Chips & guacamole	**Roasted Tomato–Basil Soup** (page 53) Grilled Black Forest ham & Gruyère sandwiches	**French Onion Soup** (page 92) Mixed salad greens with red wine vinaigrette *Pinot Noir*
Sweet Potato Soup (page 49) Spinach salad with bacon & honey-mustard vinaigrette	**Creamy Asparagus Soup** (page 77) Garlic crostini with prosciutto	

make it easy: cooking tips for soup

One of the best things about soup is its versatility: you can make it with nearly any vegetable—from peas and turnips to chard and cauliflower—and it's a great way to use up extra ingredients in the refrigerator. Use the recipes in this book as a starting point, building on them with these basic techniques and tips to create your own soups.

Prep Use a food processor to make quick work of chopping vegetables. Prep vegetables for two nights: when you are chopping vegetables for dinner, chop extra vegetables and store them in an airtight container in the refrigerator to use the next night. Keep cut-up frozen vegetables on hand to use when you don't have time to buy or prep fresh ones.

Sauté Many of the recipes in this book begin with sautéing aromatic vegetables (onions, carrots, celery) and seasonings in butter or oil to create a flavorful base for the soup. If you have a heavy soup pot or Dutch oven, you can use it for this step, then continue making the soup in the same pot.

Roast Roasting vegetables or other ingredients (beets, tomatoes, meats, poultry) before using them in soups intensifies their flavor. Because the oven does most of the work, it's a method that requires little hands-on time and delivers a big payoff.

For easy clean up, line a roasting pan with aluminum foil and brush the foil with a little olive oil to help prevent sticking. Most ingredients can be roasted a day or two ahead of time and stored in an airtight container in the refrigerator. Make extra roasted vegetables to serve on another night.

Simmer Most soups are simmered gently over low heat, requiring little attention other than occasional stirring and skimming. When making thicker soups, use a heavy-bottomed pot to avoid scorching and a wooden spoon or spatula to stir, drawing it across the bottom each time.

Purée The tall, narrow shape of a blender is ideal for puréeing mixtures with a high proportion of liquid and some chunky ingredients, making it the best tool for puréeing soups, though a food processor or immersion blender can also be used. When puréeing hot soups, fill the blender no more than two-thirds full. Cover with the lid, making sure it is secure, and then drape a kitchen towel over the lid in case there is splattering. Hold the lid down with one hand, start the motor on the slowest speed, and then increase the speed as necessary.

An immersion blender makes quick work of puréeing, and saves cleanup time because it can be used right in the soup pot. Puréeing some, but not all, of a soup is an easy way to give it a more substantial, chunky texture.

Season & enrich Season soups during cooking as directed, then taste the finished soup before serving to adjust the seasoning, adding salt and pepper as needed. Rather than simply adding them to the pot, first remove a small amount of soup, season it, and taste it to get a clearer idea of what is needed and to avoid the risk of overseasoning the whole batch.

Adding a small amount of fresh lemon juice or vinegar just before serving can brighten the flavor of many soups. Add only a few drops at a time, tasting as you go. Some soups are enriched with heavy (double) cream, sour cream, yogurt, butter, or olive oil just before serving. Stir these ingredients in gradually, and don't allow the soup to boil if you are adding sour cream or yogurt, which can curdle at high temperatures.

While you can make all of the soups in this book at any time, cooking with fresh seasonal ingredients is an easy way to guarantee great flavor and to enjoy meals that match the time of year, both the weather and the mood. Here is a guide to using the best that the season has to offer whenever you are making soup.

spring Make lightly flavored hot and chilled soups that feature delicate spring produce and other ingredients, such as asparagus, beets, Dungeness crab, fava (broad) beans, fennel, herbs (dill, chives, parsley, mint), green garlic, green (spring) onions, new potatoes, peas, and lamb.

summer Focus on chilled and hot soups that showcase the best of the harvest, including avocados, bell peppers (capsicums), chiles, corn, cucumbers, eggplants (aubergines), green beans, herbs (basil, thyme, parsley, cilantro/ fresh coriander), tomatoes, and zucchini (courgettes) and other summer squash.

autumn Put together substantial, warming soups made with slow-simmered root vegetables and other ingredients, such as broccoli, butternut squash, cauliflower, herbs (bay leaves, sage, rosemary), leeks, mushrooms (button, chanterelle, cremini, porcini), potatoes, and sweet potatoes.

winter Cook hearty soups made with meat and chunky winter vegetables and other seasonal ingredients, like beets, cabbage, fresh herbs (sage, rosemary), mushrooms, kale, parsnips, rutabagas, turnips, and winter squash such as acorn.

easy garnishes

■ **Sour cream, plain yogurt, or crème fraîche** Thin with milk or cream and, using a teaspoon, drizzle over a bowl of soup.

■ **Parmesan or aged pecorino cheese** Grate or shave directly onto a bowl of soup for the best flavor.

■ **Queso fresco** Crumble this soft, white cheese over each serving; ideal for Latin-inspired soups.

■ **Feta or blue cheese** Crumble fresh feta cheese or a mild blue cheese over each serving to add another layer of flavor.

■ **Fresh chives** Snip with kitchen scissors, allowing the bits to fall directly onto a bowl of soup.

■ **Croutons** To make your own croutons, drizzle thin slices or cubes of baguette or other crusty bread with olive oil, sprinkle with salt, and then toast in a toaster oven or on a baking sheet in a 350°F (180°C) oven until lightly browned.

■ **Fresh herbs** Strip leaves from stems and then roughly chop if necessary.

■ **Bread crumbs** Drizzle fresh bread crumbs with olive oil, sprinkle with salt, then toast in a toaster oven or in a 350°F (180°C) oven until golden.

■ **Extra-virgin olive oil** Drizzle a little fruity, bright green olive oil over each serving, making a spiral or zigzag pattern. It will add flavor and style to many Italian and other Mediterranean soups and is particularly appealing on the surface of thick vegetable purées.

■ **Salsa** Top Latin-inspired soups with a dollop of purchased salsa. If desired, add a small spoonful of sour cream topped off with a fresh cilantro (fresh coriander) leaf.

■ **Crumbled tortilla chips** Sprinkle over Latin-inspired soups to add texture and color; pass additional crumbled chips at the table.

■ **Crumbled bacon** Brown some extra bacon when cooking it for a soup base, then chop and sprinkle over each serving.

shop smarter

Using only the freshest produce and other high-quality ingredients will give you a head start toward great flavor and healthier eating. Try to patronize a butcher, fishmonger, produce store, and market that carry first-rate items and deliver personalized service. Call ahead and place your order, so it is ready to pick up on your way home from work.

■ **Broth & stock** Most of the recipes in this book call for purchased chicken, beef, or vegetable broth. The reason is simple: using these commercial products is the best way to make quick and easy soups. Good-quality broths can be found in cans and aseptic boxes on market shelves. Read the labels carefully to avoid unwholesome ingredients and, if possible, purchase organic brands for both better flavor and health. Many specialty food shops sell their own made-from-scratch fresh or frozen stocks, which are another good option. If you have time to make your own, homemade stocks will deliver a big difference in flavor, which is why recipes for several stocks have been included in the Make More to Store chapter.

■ **Produce** When visiting the market, ask which fruits and vegetables are at their peak of flavor and ripeness. Buy precut vegetables, such as broccoli crowns, as well as prewashed vegetables, such as spinach or salad greens, to save on prep time. If there is a regular farmers' market in your area, get in the habit of visiting it once a week. It's an excellent way to stay in touch with what is in season, and you'll often find good deals on bumper-crop produce.

■ **Meat & poultry** Look for meat with good, uniform color and a fresh smell. Any fat should be bright white rather than grayish. Poultry should be plump, with smooth skin and firm flesh, and any visible fat should be white to light yellow. If you need boned meat or poultry, ask the butcher to do it for you, to save you time in the kitchen.

■ **Seafood** Look for fish and shellfish with bright color, a moist surface, and little or no "fishy" smell. Ask the purveyor which fish and shellfish are freshest. If possible, use seafood the same day you purchase it.

MAKE A SHOPPING LIST

prepare in advance Make a list of what you need to buy before you go shopping and you'll save time at the store.

make a template Create a list template on your computer, then fill it in during the week before you go shopping.

categorize your lists Use the following categories to keep your lists organized: pantry, fresh, and occasional.

■ **pantry items** Check the pantry and write down any items that need to be restocked to make the meals on your weekly plan.

■ **fresh ingredients** These are for immediate use and include produce, seafood, meats, and some cheeses. You might need to visit different stores or supermarket sections, so divide the list into subcategories, such as produce, dairy, and meats.

■ **occasional items** This is a revolving list for refrigerated items that are replaced as needed, such as butter and milk.

be flexible Be ready to change your menus based on the freshest ingredients at the market.

SAMPLE SHOPPING LIST

PANTRY ITEMS

canned black beans

chicken broth

croutons

long-grain rice

olive oil

peppercorns

soy sauce

FRESH: PRODUCE

asparagus

bok choy

button mushrooms

carrots

celery

flat-leaf (Italian) parsley

leeks

russet potatoes

tomatoes

FRESH: MEATS & SEAFOOD

boneless pork loin

bacon

shrimp (prawns)

FRESH: DAIRY

Cheddar cheese

heavy (double) cream

queso fresco

sour cream

OCCASIONAL ITEMS

milk

unsalted butter

use shortcut ingredients

Whatever you are cooking, certain ingredients can make the job easier and save prep time, either because they are precooked or because they add concentrated, intense flavor. Here are some time-saving soup ingredients.

- **Canned beans** Save soaking and simmering time with canned beans. Always discard the liquid and rinse the beans well before using.

- **Rotisserie chicken** Buy enough chicken for dinner one night, plus leftovers, and cut up the leftover meat to add to soup the next night. Save the carcass and refrigerate or freeze, and then use it to enrich purchased chicken broth.

- **Cooked sausages** Slice fully cooked sausages, such as andouille, smoked chorizo, chicken with apple, or kielbasa, and add directly to soups, or brown first for extra flavor.

- **Frozen vegetables** Keep a supply of frozen peas, mixed Italian-style vegetables, and corn on hand to spruce up a variety of soups.

- **Canned tomatoes** Use canned tomatoes rather than out-of-season fresh tomatoes for better flavor. Because they are already peeled, you'll save kitchen time, too.

- **Tomato or tomato-vegetable juice** Use these everyday juices as a base for hot or cold soups to save time and intensify flavor.

- **Herbes de Provence** This aromatic blend of dried herbs is a one-step ingredient that balances the flavors of several dried herbs.

- **Dried mushrooms** The concentrated flavor of dried porcini, shiitake, or other mushrooms complements many soups. To reconstitute, place the mushrooms in a heatproof bowl, cover with boiling water, cover the bowl, and soak until soft and flexible, at least 10 minutes. Remove the mushrooms and chop, discarding any woody stems. Strain the soaking liquid to remove any grit and add to soups for flavor.

- **Tomato paste** Buy tomato paste in a tube and refrigerate after opening. Add a small amount to soups to intensify flavor.

the well-stocked kitchen

Smart cooking is all about being prepared. Keeping your pantry, refrigerator, and freezer well stocked and organized means you'll always save time when you are ready to cook. Get into the habit of regularly keeping track of what is in your kitchen and you'll find you can shop less frequently and spend less time in the store.

What follows is a guide to the ingredients you'll need to have on hand to make a variety of soups, along with tips on how to organize and store them efficiently. Check to see what is in your kitchen now, so you know what you need to buy; then all you'll have to do is make a few lists, do some strategic shopping, and fill your shelves. Once your kitchen is stocked and organized, you'll be able to make any soup in this book by picking up just a few fresh ingredients.

the pantry

The pantry is typically a closet or one or more cupboards in which you store dried herbs and spices, pasta and egg noodles, canned goods, and such fresh ingredients as garlic, onions, shallots, and any root vegetables that don't require refrigeration. Make sure that it is relatively cool, dry, dark when not in use, and away from the heat of the stove, which can hasten spoilage.

stock your pantry

- Take inventory of what is in your pantry using the Pantry Staples list.

- Remove everything from the pantry; clean the shelves and reline with paper, if needed; and then resort the items by type.

- Discard items that have passed their expiration date or have a stale or otherwise questionable appearance.

- Make a list of items that you need to replace or stock.

- Shop for the items on your list.

- Restock the pantry, organizing items by type so everything is easy to find.

- Write the purchase date on perishable items and clearly label bulk items.

- Keep staples you use often toward the front of the pantry.

- Keep dried herbs and spices each in its own container and preferably in a separate spice or herb organizer, shelf, or drawer.

keep it organized

- Look over the recipes in your weekly meal plan and check your pantry to make sure you have all the ingredients you'll need.

- Rotate items as you use them, moving the oldest ones to the front of the pantry so they will be used first.

- Keep a list of the items you use up so that you can replace them.

USING DRIED HERBS

Fresh herbs, with their bright taste, are generally the best choice for flavoring soups, but some dried herbs can be used successfully, including rosemary, thyme, marjoram, oregano, and sage.

The flavor of dried herbs is concentrated, so always use a smaller amount of the dried herb than the fresh. To substitute dried for fresh, use the following:

1 teaspoon dried tarragon or sage = 1 tablespoon fresh

2 teaspoons dried oregano, marjoram, or thyme = 1 tablespoon fresh

1 ½ teaspoons dried rosemary = 1 tablespoon fresh

BUYING BROTH

The busy cook seldom has time to make homemade stock, but good-quality chicken, beef, and vegetable broth can be found in cans or aseptic boxes on market shelves, or in containers in the frozen-food section of many upscale markets, delis, and some butchers.

PANTRY STORAGE

dried herbs & spices Buy in small quantities, store in airtight containers, and use within 6 months, after which they will have lost their potency.

oils Store unopened bottles of oil at room temperature in a cool, dark place. Although oils will keep for up to 1 year, their flavor diminishes over time. Once a bottle is opened, store for 3 months at room temperature or in the refrigerator for several months. Taste or smell oils to make sure they are not rancid before using them. (Because nut oils spoil much faster than other types, they should be stored in the refrigerator once opened.)

grains & dried pastas Store grains in airtight containers for up to 3 months, checking occasionally for signs of rancidity or infestation. The shelf life of most dried pastas is 1 year. Although they are safe to eat beyond that time, they will have lost flavor and can become brittle. Once you break the seal on a package, slip what you don't cook into a resealable storage bag or an airtight container and return to the shelf.

fresh foods Store fresh foods in a cool, dark place and check occasionally for signs of sprouting or spoilage. Never put potatoes alongside onions; when placed next to each other, they produce gases that hasten spoilage.

canned foods Discard canned foods if the can shows any signs of expansion or buckling. Once you have opened a can, transfer the unused contents to an airtight container and refrigerate or freeze.

PANTRY STAPLES

DRIED HERBS & SPICES

bay leaves

black peppercorns

cayenne pepper

chili powder

cinnamon sticks

coriander seeds

cumin

curry powder

filé powder

ground cumin

ground turmeric

herbes de Provence

oregano

paprika

red pepper flakes

salt

thyme

white pepper

OILS & VINEGARS

Asian sesame oil

canola oil

olive oil

red wine vinegar

SPIRITS

dry white & red wine

vermouth

MISCELLANEOUS

flour

pecans

sugar

GRAINS, PASTAS & LEGUMES

egg noodles

lentils

long-grain white rice

orzo or other short soup pasta

pearl barley

quinoa

rice vermicelli

soba noodles

CANNED & PACKAGED FOODS

broth: beef, chicken & vegetable

black beans

cannellini beans

chickpeas (garbanzo beans)

chipotle chiles in adobo

coconut milk

Asian fish sauce

plum (Roma) tomatoes

soy sauce

tomato juice

tomato paste

FRESH FOODS

baguette

garlic

lemons

limes

potatoes

red onions

shallots

sweet potatoes

yellow onions

the refrigerator & freezer

Once you have stocked and organized your pantry, you can apply the same time-saving principles to your refrigerator and freezer. Used for short-term cold storage, the refrigerator is ideal for storing your homemade chicken, beef, and vegetable stock and leftover soup. Done properly, freezing will preserve most of the flavor and nutrients in certain soups and is especially recommended for storing stock.

general tips

- Foods lose flavor under refrigeration, so proper storage and an even temperature of below 40°F (5°C) are important.

- Freeze foods at 0°F (-18°C) or below to retain color, texture, and flavor.

- Never crowd foods in the refrigerator or freezer. You want air to circulate freely to keep refrigerated foods evenly cooled and to freeze foods quickly, which helps preserve their flavor.

- To prevent freezer burn, use only moistureproof wrappings such as aluminum foil, airtight plastic containers, or resealable plastic bags.

soup & stock storage

- Let stocks and soups cool to room temperature, then transfer to airtight containers. Refrigerate stocks and most soups for up to 4 days.

- In general, bean, tomato, and broth-based soups and all stocks are good candidates for freezing.

- To freeze soups and stocks, let cool to room temperature and transfer to an airtight container, leaving 1 inch (2.5 cm) headroom to allow for expansion during freezing. Alternatively, pack in a resealable plastic freezer bag. Label and date the container or freezer bag and then freeze soups for up to 1 month and stocks for up to 3 months.

- Freeze soups in small batches sized for 1 or 2 servings. These are great for a quick, healthy meal.

KEEP IT ORGANIZED

clean first Remove items a few at a time and wash the refrigerator thoroughly with warm, soapy water, then rinse well with clear water. Wash and rinse your freezer at the same time.

rotate items Check the expiration dates on refrigerated items and discard any that have exceeded their time. Also, toss out any items that look questionable.

stock up Use the list at the right as a starting point to decide what you need to buy or replace.

shop Shop for the items on your list.

date of purchase Label items that you plan to keep for more than a few weeks, writing the date directly on the package.

THAWING STOCK & SOUP

To thaw frozen stock or soup, transfer the container to the refrigerator for 24 hours.

Or, to thaw it quickly, place the frozen block in a saucepan and warm it over low heat until liquefied.

fresh herb & vegetable storage

- Trim the stem ends of a bunch of parsley, stand the bunch in a glass of water, drape a plastic bag loosely over the leaves, and refrigerate. Wrap other fresh herbs in a damp paper towel, slip into a plastic bag, and store in the crisper. Rinse and stem all herbs just before using.

- Store tomatoes and eggplants (aubergines) at room temperature.

- Cut about ½ inch (12 mm) off the end of each asparagus spear, stand the spears, tips up, in a glass of cold water, and refrigerate, changing the water daily. The asparagus will keep for up to 1 week.

- Rinse leafy greens, such as chard, spin dry in a salad spinner, wrap in damp paper towels, and store in a resealable plastic bag in the crisper for up to 1 week. In general, store other vegetables in resealable bags in the crisper and rinse before using. Sturdy vegetables will keep for up to a week; more delicate ones will keep for only a few days.

cheese storage

- Wrap all cheeses well to prevent them from drying out. Hard cheeses, such as Parmesan, have a low moisture content, so they keep longer than fresh cheeses, such as *queso fresco*. Use fresh cheeses within a couple days. Store soft and semisoft cheeses for up to 2 weeks, and hard cheeses for up to 1 month.

meat, poultry & seafood storage

- Most seafood should be used the same day you purchase it. Place clams or mussels in a bowl, cover with a damp towel, and use within a day.

- Use fresh meat and poultry within 2 days of purchase. If buying packaged meats, check the expiration date and use before that date.

- Place packaged meats on a plate in the coldest part of the refrigerator. If only part of a package is used, discard the original wrapping and rewrap in fresh wrapping.

index

OXMOOR HOUSE

Oxmoor House books are distributed by Sunset Books
80 Willow Road, Menlo Park, CA 94025
Telephone: 650 321 3600 Fax: 650 324 1532

Vice President/General Manager Rich Smeby
National Accounts Manager/Special Sales Brad Moses
Oxmoor House and Sunset Books are divisions of
Southern Progress Corporation

WILLIAMS-SONOMA
Founder & Vice-Chairman Chuck Williams

THE WILLIAMS-SONOMA FOOD MADE FAST SERIES
Conceived and produced by Weldon Owen Inc.
814 Montgomery Street, San Francisco, CA 94133
Telephone: 415 291 0100 Fax: 415 291 8841

In collaboration with Williams-Sonoma, Inc.
3250 Van Ness Avenue, San Francisco, CA 94109

Photographer Bill Bettencourt
Food Stylist Kevin Crafts
Photographer's Assistant Emily Polar
Food Stylist's Assistants Luis Bustamante, Alexa Hyman
Prop Stylist Robin Turk
Text Writer Steve Siegelman

Library of Congress Cataloging-in-Publication data is available.
ISBN 0-8487-3136-0

WELDON OWEN INC.

Chief Executive Officer John Owen
President and Chief Operating Officer Terry Newell
Chief Financial Officer Christine E. Munson
Vice President International Sales Stuart Laurence
Creative Director Gaye Allen
Publisher Hannah Rahill
Art Director Kyrie Forbes Panton
Senior Editor Kim Goodfriend
Editor Emily Miller
Designers Andrea Stephany, Kelly Booth
Assistant Editor Juli Vendzules
Production Director Chris Hemesath
Color Manager Teri Bell
Production and Reprint Coordinator Todd Rechner

A WELDON OWEN PRODUCTION
Copyright © 2006 by Weldon Owen Inc. and Williams-Sonoma, Inc.
All rights reserved, including the right of reproduction in
whole or in part in any form.

Set in Formata
First printed in 2006
10 9 8 7 6 5 4 3 2 1
Color separations by Bright Arts Singapore
Printed by Tien Wah Press

Printed in Singapore

ACKNOWLEDGMENTS
Weldon Owen wishes to thank the following people for their generous support in producing this book:
Davina Baum, Heather Belt, Carrie Bradley, Ken DellaPenta, Judith Dunham, Marianne Mitten,
Sharon Silva, and Kate Washington.

Photographs by Tucker + Hossler: pages 94 and 102

Cover photograph by Tucker + Hossler: Sweet Potato Soup, page 49

A NOTE ON WEIGHTS AND MEASURES
All recipes include customary U.S. and metric measurements. Metric conversions are based on
a standard developed for these books and have been rounded off. Actual weights may vary.